Charles Brooks And His Work For Normal Schools

John Albree

CHARLES BROOKS

And His Work for Normal Schools

BY

JOHN ALBREE

READ BEFORE THE MEDFORD HISTORICAL SOCIETY
May fifth, 1906

PRESS OF J. C. MILLER, JR.
MEDFORD, MASS.
1907

gift of

Rev. CHARLES BROOKS (1795–1872),

Pastor of Third Parish, Hingham.

Painting by Frothingham, 1825, in possession of the Medford Historical Society.

A WORD seems needed to justify printing a paper relating to a work which was completed seventy years ago. Charles Brooks himself showed a singular reticence about his labors, the reason for which has not clearly appeared.* Consequently, among his Medford friends and neighbors, Brooks' part in the educational revival was not understood, and with the lapse of time such ideas as did exist, became vague. To set forth the facts therefore this paper was prepared and read before a company of Medford people, some of whom as children had known Mr. Brooks, and on their request it is now submitted to a wider circle.

JOHN ALBREE.

SWAMPSCOTT, MASSACHUSETTS,
     January 1, 1907.

---

* Brooks' *Medford*, p. 285.

REPRINTED FROM THE "HISTORICAL REGISTER,"
VOL. X, No. 1, JANUARY, 1907, PUBLISHED BY
THE MEDFORD HISTORICAL SOCIETY

CHARLES BROOKS *and his* WORK *for* NORMAL SCHOOLS

By way of prelude let me ask if the traditions will be violated if a text is chosen, especially if it is agreed that the text will not again be referred to? This is necessary by reason of the comments that have been made by some on learning that a paper was in preparation on " Charles Brooks and His Work for Normal Schools." These comments, more or less diplomatic and guarded, have been to the effect that the name of Horace Mann ought to appear in the title.

The text is " One star differeth from another star in glory."

ON a summer afternoon, how many years ago is not material, a baby was a member of a little party that called at the home of the Brooks family in Medford, a home that by reason of its furnishings and surroundings was entitled to be called the Brooks Mansion. Nothing could have been further from the minds of that household than that in the future that baby, when grown to manhood, was to stand before a Medford audience of Medford people and submit for consideration a paper on their " Brother Charles," for that was the way he was always addressed, in the delightfully formal manner characteristic of their home life. Furthermore, that in such a paper it would be assumed at the outset that neither Charles Brooks nor his work would then be known in Medford, their Medford, and that the time would then have arrived when they, both brothers and sisters, would well nigh have passed from the memory of living men.

At times it seems to have come over Charles Brooks that perhaps his three years of hard, though ultimately successful work might not have secured a firm place in history. In 1845, we find that in a letter giving an account of his labors he tried to forecast the future. He indulged in a little fancy and said, "Some educational antiquary, in his pardonable weakness, may show my lectures fifty years hence as they sometimes show old cannon."* And tonight the thought of sixty years ago becomes a fact. While perhaps the title of "educational antiquary" hardly applies to your essayist, it will be assumed and the results of the delving recounted. Fortunately a valuable clew to the situation was found, and through the thoughtfulness of Mrs. Sarah Warner Brooks important, original material, a scrap-book, of Brooks' was found. Without this book, so carefully prepared, this paper must have been based on evidence at second hand and of doubtful authenticity. As it is, we are able to hear Charles Brooks' own words, and to examine cotemporary evidence in support of his statements.

When the educational revival had been in progress for twenty-five years, and teachers and educators had appreciated the magnificence of the undertaking, it seemed to them to be well to hold a meeting at which the historical features might be treated. It was to this meeting that Charles Brooks was invited. The record of the meeting is most valuable, for here we find at first hand the stories of those concerned, and the particular work of each is described.

The invitation Brooks received was from the committee, that he attend "The Quarter Centennial Normal School Celebration at Framingham, July 1, 1864." The secretary, George N. Bigelow, added a few lines to the printed form which are suggestive.

" It seems best that we should hear from your own lips something of the work that you did in the establishing of Normal Schools. . . . I am sorry that I was so ignorant of your great labors in this work of Normal Schools. But then, when you were so gloriously engaged, I was just entering my teens, and what should a mere boy be expected to know of what you have so long kept in silence for the sake of your children?"

*Old Colony Memorial Newspaper, Plymouth. October 4, 1845.

Brooks accepted the invitation and made an address in which he reviewed his work.* This review will be considered later in its course, but it is referred to at this time because it shows that, in using the scrap-book in the compilation of this paper, we are doing what Brooks expected would be done at some time. Picture to yourselves, therefore, this slightly built, elderly man, with a winning smile and charming manner, standing before that audience over twoscore of years ago and beginning his address with these words, for they show how he felt, and they corroborate a statement in the Bigelow letter about his keeping silence: —

"Mr. President: I am called to a position which I have tried to avoid. For more than a quarter of a century I have kept a profound silence concerning my connection with the introduction of the present system of State Normal Schools in New England, and should have kept silence to the end, had not this noble, patriotic, and Christian celebration induced some friends to tempt me to break that silence, averring it injustice to withhold the facts.

"It happens that I alone possess all the historical documents, and I have used them in writing a history of one hundred and sixty-eight pages concerning the public movements in 1835 to 1838, not for publication, but as a legacy to my children. I have carefully preserved in one large quarto volume all the manuscript, documentary evidence, and in a folio, all the printed evidence of the facts I have stated, carefully noting dates and places.

"Now can you imagine anything more ridiculous and contradictory than for a *living* man to stand up here and read his *posthumous* histories? Has God opened a seam in the dark cloud of the grave that he may send one ray of light to increase the full-orbed joy of this sacred occasion?"

You note that he mentions three books he prepared, but of them only one, the last mentioned, has come to light. The manuscript history and the volume of manuscript documentary evidence have eluded discovery, but the folio of the printed evidence, with dates and places carefully noted, is before you.

He began the book as a "Common place Book," using

*History of Missionary Agency of the State Normal Schools of Prussia in Massachusetts in 1835-6-7 and 8. Read at the Quarter Centennial Normal School Celebration in Framingham, Massachusetts, July 1, 1864, by Rev. Charles Brooks, Medford. Boston Evening Transcript, July 13, 1864. Also, printed by request: not published. Boston, John Wilson & Son, 1864.

it for sundry scraps and clippings.   Later, some of these earlier scraps were covered with others of later date.   In addition, there is the usual miscellaneous assortment of scraps having no connection with each other.   Whatever he wrote that had appeared in the papers he has preserved, also, any mention of him was duly clipped and inserted.

There are some family scraps, tax bills, etc.   Here is a bill rendered his great great grandfather,Cochran Reeve, in 1738, for expenses on account of a slave.   The items are specified as freight, nursing, and a coffin.   The jailors's bill had not been received, so that could not be included.   But for our present purpose we find many clippings which will be referred to from time to time.

It is a strange sensation to study, not to glance hastily, but to study a scrap-book, especially such a personal one as this.   In our own experience we find ourselves at times perplexed as to why we preserved some clipping.   It was probably Brooks' experience as well.   And yet, after reading what he said about the " educational antiquary," one is struck with these lines, pasted just below his printed signature on a circular regarding the Clergyman's Aid Society.   It seems as if he may have again been looking into the future.

CONSOLING.
You 'll be forgotten as old debts
    By persons who are used to borrow;
Forgotten as the sun that sets
    When shines a new one on the morrow.
Forgotten, like the luscious peach
    That blessed the school boy last September;
Forgotten, like a maiden speech
    Which all men praise, but none remember.

But later he wrote these lines, when he was in a reminiscent mood, and dated them 1865.

And though some hopes I cherished once
    Died most untimely in their birth,
Yet I have been beloved and blest
    Beyond the measure of my worth.

CHARLES BROOKS (1795–1872),

AT ELEVEN YEARS. 1806.

Silhouette by King, a deservedly famous silhouettist of the period.

The question arose as to how fully these clippings represented the newspaper accounts of Brooks' work, and so it seemed well to examine a file of a cotemporary newspaper. The Hingham paper was selected, as that was the paper of his town, and the result showed that Brooks clipped and preserved in the scrap-book practically all the references to himself that appeared in the paper. Mr. Brooks relied on the press for much help during his active work, but the methods of that day were much different from those of ours. There was not the appeal to the interest of all classes and conditions of men; the reading public seems to have been limited in numbers. But there have been many changes in thought and life during the seventy years that have elapsed since Charles Brooks was doing his grand work of bringing to the common people of Massachusetts a remedy for their great needs, and these changes must be considered before taking up directly what Brooks did.

For instance, in the '30s an assemblage of the gentle sex was denominated a company of females. To this appellation some bright mind would venture a protest, but the custom was too firmly established to be set aside because some lone "female" objected.

Again, suppose it were now printed on a notice that Harvard College sent to members of a committee, announcing that a meeting would be held, "Gentlemen will please to select their own method of conveyance and charge the expense to the University." Such a note Mr. Brooks received. When one sees it he wonders how many different methods there were for reaching Cambridge, which was the most used, and what was the expenditure of time and money.

Or again, what is there in the statement, "As is the teacher, so is the school," that endangers the established order, or that is revolutionary in its character? Any man who would now hesitate to subscribe to that statement, "As is the teacher, so is the school," would find it difficult to get a hearing for his doubts. Yet it was to impress this truth on the thinking and acting minds of his day that Charles Brooks gave unsparingly of his time, his money, and his strength.

If it were not for these changes in thought and life, it would suffice to read the Framingham address, which in 1864 Brooks delivered on his work, its methods, and results. It is written in his characteristic style, simple, frank, and attractive, but unless one can get at the general thought of the time, the difficulties, the obstacles, the discouragements, and the triumphs, the address, if read without comment, would serve to arouse, but not to satisfy, inquiry. To meet this inquiry, to supply some comment, and to define Brooks' part in the great educational revival, is the purpose of this paper.

If we briefly summarize what Mr. Brooks' life had been prior to undertaking this work, we may be able to form a better conception of his personality, for this attractive personality was a predominating feature in his success. Few of those who knew him now remain, except such as knew him in his later years. It has been interesting to record the epithets these use in describing him. Genial is always the first, and then affable, pleasant, entertaining, sympathetic, industrious, are other words used to formulate the impression those who knew him have retained all these years. As the story of his work is told, we shall be able to see reasons for using words descriptive of deeper, stronger, and more abiding traits of character which will be discerned on a closer acquaintance.

He was born in the ancient house still standing at the corner of High and Woburn streets, October 30, 1795. He was fitted for Harvard under Dr. Luther Stearns, who came to Medford as a teacher, but who occasionally practised medicine. He became a member of the class of 1816 at Harvard.

The scrap-book contains a little relic of the student life of long ago. Napoleon Bonaparte was an object that

REV. CHARLES BROOKS (1795–1872),
HINGHAM, 1821.

Silhouette in colors, artist unknown.

loomed large in the eyes of the world. He had just been sent to Saint Helena, and the question was whether he could escape. We find that two students expressed their beliefs in this record of a wager. There is no record whether the dinner was held.

" Bet with C. Brooks that Napoleon Bonaparte will escape from the Island of St. Helena before the first of August, A.D., 1819; a good dinner at our class meeting.
"November 12, 1815. SAM'L D. BELL."*

This date in August, 1819, was chosen because that was the month in which Commencement exercises were then held. Brooks took good rank in his course, and on graduation continued his theological studies at Harvard. In the month mentioned in the record of the wager he took his Master's degree and delivered the valedictory in Latin. This paper is still preserved.

In November, 1820, he was invited to become pastor of the Third Church at Hingham at a salary of a thousand dollars, and here he remained until January, 1839, a period of eighteen years. Time permits only the mention of the activities of this enthusiastic young pastor, who did not confine his work alone to his church and his parish. And in these enterprises and undertakings he was the leader. The first year of his ministry he wrote a family prayer book, of which there were eighteen editions published. A Boston merchant bought two thousand copies, which in 1846 he had distributed widely through the publishers, the donor's name not being given.

He established a Sunday-school — then a novel feature — a parish reading society, was the founder and secretary of the Old Colony Peace Society. In fact, he appears to have been the secretary in most of the societies with which he was connected. He was active in the Plymouth County Bible Society, and the year he

*One of the last clippings Brooks inserted in the scrap book was an obituary notice of his college friend, Bell. Samuel Dana Bell (1797-1868) was a son of Governor Samuel Bell of New Hampshire. He studied law and practiced in Concord and Manchester. In 1859 he was appointed Chief Justice of the Supreme Judicial Court. He resigned in 1865 and died at Manchester July, 1868.

was abroad the work languished seriously. He advocated the establishment of the Hingham Institution for Savings, which still continues on its prosperous course. The account* of his introduction of anthracite coal into Hingham is preserved, telling how some of his friends were fearful for the safety of the Brooks household with "those red hot stones" in the house at night. He agitated successfully for the establishment of the Hingham and Boston steamboat line, and generally he made his influence felt for the good of the community.†

Meanwhile he married and had three children born, one of whom died in infancy. And it is not to be wondered at, therefore, that under these varied achievements, requiring so much time, strength, and ardent endeavor, his health began to fail and rest was needed. So, in 1833, he went to Europe, sailing November 1, 1833, in ship *Erie* from New York.

There are suggestions in the scrap-book and in his writings of experiences he had, and of people‡ he met on this journey, whose names are now household names. For instance, there is one clipping giving the story of his meeting Felicia Hemans, the author of the old Pilgrim hymn. His letters were carefully kept and then bound in one volume. He was untiring in his sight seeing and painstaking in reporting all he saw.

From this brief recital we can obtain some conception of Charles Brooks, his personality, his characteristics, his capacity for work, and of the success which resulted. Now we must be allowed an inference that in all these activities, he could not but have appreciated the conditions of schools and of general education. Let us leave him for a while on his European trip, while we see what he must have seen, and what others certainly saw regarding the condition of schools.

There are four who are competent authorities as to the condition of teachers and schools at this time. The

*Hingham Journal, March 4, 1862. History of Hingham, Vol. I, Part II, p. 52.
†Memoir of Rev. Charles Brooks, by Solomon Lincoln of Hingham. Proceedings Massachusetts Historical Society, June, 1880.
‡ " I have letters to Miss Edgeworth, Mrs. Hemans, Miss Lucy Aiken, Miss Martineau, the Bishop of London, Lafayette, etc., etc." Letter of Brooks to his wife, October 31, 1833.

first is James G. Carter, whose work will be later spoken of. In a paper,* published in 1824, he described the teachers of the primary summer schools as "possessed of very moderate attainments, for they were often very young, constantly changing their employment, and consequently with but little experience." He asks "if there is any *other* service in which young and often ignorant persons are employed, without some previous instruction in their appropriate duties." You wonder how such teachers were appointed, and Carter explains. He says, "No standard of attainments is fixed at which these female teachers must arrive before they assume the business of instruction, so that any one KEEPS *school* (which is a very different thing from TEACHING *school*), who wishes to do it and can persuade, by herself or her friends, a small district to employ her."

Professor Francis Bowen† of Harvard, writing fifty years ago of the common school system of New England, said that at this time — the early 'thirties —"it had degenerated into routine, it was starved by parsimony. Any hovel would answer for a schoolhouse, any primer would do for a text-book, any farmer's apprentice was competent to keep school."

George H. Martin, the present secretary of the Board of Education, and therefore a successor of Horace Mann, in his book which has become a standard, "The Evolution of the Massachusetts Public School System," says,‡ "The majority of Massachusetts citizens were torpid, so far as school interests were concerned, or if aroused at all, awakened only to a spasmodic and momentary excitement over the building of a new chimney to a district schoolhouse, or the adding of a half-dollar a month to the wages of a school-mistress."

And the fourth is Brooks himself. In his address before the American Institute of Instruction, at Worces-

*The Schools of Massachusetts in 1824, by James Gordon Carter. Old South Leaflets, No. 135.
†Memoir of Edmund Dwight, by Francis Bowen. Barnard's Journal of Education, Vol. IV, p. 14, September, 1857.
‡The Evolution of the Massachusetts Public School System: a Historical Sketch, by George H. Martin, A.M., Supervisor of Public Schools, Boston. New York, D. Appleton & Co., 1904. P. 146.

ter, August, 1837, he quoted from a petition to the Legislature the previous winter, and said, " The committee of the institute in their petition gave their evidence before the world in these words, ' A very large number of both sexes who teach the summer and winter schools are to a mournful degree wanting in all these qualifications, in short, they know not *what* to teach, nor *how* to teach, nor in *what spirit* to teach, nor what is the *nature* of those they undertake to lead, nor what they are *themselves* to stand forward to lead them.'"

I will not ask you to burden your minds with these quotations, for it is certain that some of the words will stay by you, such as, "young and ignorant persons," "starved by parsimony," "hovel," "farmer's apprentice," "excitement about new chimney." These conditions, mind you, were in Massachusetts, not in some border territory or frontier settlement, and the time was the third and fourth decades of the last century.

But it must not be supposed that all were indifferent to the existence of such deplorable conditions. The work of these men is fully discussed by Dr. Hinsdale in his " Life of Horace Mann,"* in the chapter on " Horace Mann's Forerunners." In this he aims "to name the principal of Mr. Mann's precursors, and briefly to characterize their work." The bibliography of the educational work is large and complete, and an investigator will find much that will interest him if he compares and contrasts the plans proposed. But in such a paper as this, which treats of the definite work of Charles Brooks, it would be wandering from the subject and would tend to confusion if an attempt were made to treat of the general work and of what others were doing, except as such work was related to that which Brooks marked out to be done by himself. Brooks did a definite and specific work. Its inception, its progress, and its consummation, all are clearly defined.

That Brooks did have a clear and definite purpose

*Horace Mann and the Common School Revival in the United States, by B.A. Hinsdale, Ph.D. LL.D.   Professor of the Science and the Art of Teaching in the University of Michigan. New York, Chas. Scribner's Sons, 1898.

for which he was striving during these years is shown by the fact that he knew when his object was attained. Note his statement in the Framingham address, when he reviewed his great work. He briefly stated his purpose and its accomplishment in these words, " The Prussian system with its two central powers, a board of education and normal schools, was not known in New England, when I first described it in public in 1835, but on the 19th of April, 1838, Massachusetts, the Banner State, adopted State Normal Schools by statute. . . . The 19th of April, 1838, has ever since been a red letter day in my memory."

Mr. Brooks' statement that the Prussian system was not known in New England is confirmed by the researches of Dr. Hinsdale, whose conclusion we can adopt. He found that " down to 1835, there is no direct evidence showing that American educators were acquainted with what had been done in Europe for the training of teachers."*

There had been, however, from time to time, expressions more or less formal, that teachers should be fitted for their work, for the reason that teaching is a profession, and requires special training, as does any other profession. There was an appreciation of the fact that schools might be improved, and suggestions had been offered as to how to bring about the desired result. Not only in Massachusetts, but in Connecticut, New York, and Pennsylvania, were there those who were thinking, talking, and planning, but no practicable result had as yet been reached.

In later years, after Massachusetts showed the way, and proved by results its effectiveness, other states followed. It has been pointed out by Dr. W. T. Harris, late United States Commissioner of Education, that while state pride usually leads to the choice of one's own state to head the list in educational history, uniformly the second place is assigned to Massachusetts.†

*Hinsdale's Horace Mann, pp. 146-7.
†Martin's Massachusetts Public School System, Editor's Preface.

There is one name that stands out above all others in the early years of the educational revival, that is, prior to 1837, James G. Carter of Lancaster, Massachusetts. A Harvard graduate of 1820, a teacher by profession, a clear, strong thinker, and a forcible writer, he began as early as 1824 to publish to the world his thoughts on the Principles of Instruction. Then he sought to reach the public through the columns of a Boston newspaper, and suggested an outline of an institution for the education of teachers. His ideas were new, attracted much attention, and were discussed in the periodicals of the time. He was active in founding the American Institute of Instruction, in 1830, an organization that still exists in a flourishing condition, thus proving Carter's appreciation of what was needed. Later, as a member of the Legislature, he strove earnestly for the cause of education, as we shall see presently.*

But there was one thing lacking to set the work going, namely, the arousing of public sentiment to demand action that would lead to better teachers and better schools, and to this work, for which he was especially adapted, Charles Brooks gave three of the best years of his life.

Now we left Mr. Brooks a while ago, sailing for Europe in 1833. Let us return to him and hear him tell in his own words how he was led to take up this work.†

"At a literary soiree in London, August, 1834, I met Dr. H. Julius of Hamburg, then on his way to the United States, having been sent by the King of Prussia to learn the condition of our schools, hospitals, prisons, and other public institutions. He asked to be my room-mate on board ship. I was too happy to accede to that request. A passage of forty-one days from Liverpool to New York gave me time to ask all manner of questions concerning the noble, philosophical and practical system of Prussian elementary education. He explained it like a sound scholar and a pious Christian. If you will allow the phrase, I fell in love with the Prussian system, and it seemed to possess me like a missionary angel. I gave myself to it, and in the Gulf Stream I resolved to

*Barnards Journal of Education, Vol. V, pp. 407-416; also Hinsdale's Mann. p. 52; Martin's Public School System, p. 147.
†Framingham Address.

do something about *State* normal schools. This was its birth in me, and I baptized it my Seaborn School.

"After this I looked upon each child as a being who could complain of me before God if I refused to provide for him a better education, after what I had learned."

Six months later, that is, in the spring of 1835, Dr. Julius made a visit to Mr. Brooks at Hingham, and Brooks announced that he was going to make the attempt to introduce the Prussian system into Massachusetts.

It is evident that he recognized the importance of having a thorough preparation for the campaign, for in addition to his other studies, he corresponded with Victor Cousin, whom he had met upon his European journey. Cousin's work on the Prussian system of normal schools had already been translated into English, and was meeting with favor in the circles where the matter of improved educational facilities was the subject of deep concern.

When Brooks felt that he had learned his story, he wrote and published, but in his own words, " Few read and still fewer felt any interest. I was considered a dreamer, who wished to fill our Republican Commonwealth with monarchical institutions."

But Brooks' whole active life showed that he was not one to be turned aside from his purpose, if he had made up his mind that the idea for which he was working was right. If one plan did not bring the desired result, then others were devised. And, as by the printing press he did not obtain his results,* he determined to try the effect of his personal presence and his word of mouth. On Thanksgiving Day, 1835, he delivered a carefully prepared address to his people of Hingham, setting forth at length and in detail, the needs of the schools in general, and particularly, what the Prussian system of State normal schools, if adopted, would accomplish in Massa-

*Christian Register, Dec. 27, 1834, "Schools." This article, unsigned, Brooks clipped and initialled in the scrap book. There are also unsigned articles, June 22 and July 11, 1835, on Public Instruction of Prussia, which are in Brooks' style.

chusetts. He dwelt on the phrase which he used so often, " As is the teacher, so is the school."

He had hoped that there would be a request that this sermon be printed, but none came. Nevertheless, he found some encouragement, so that he was satisfied that by address and discussion he could best further the cause. Accordingly he prepared three lectures. He says himself they are enormously long, two hours each. The first described minutely the Prussian system. In the second, he showed how it could be adapted to conditions in Massachusetts, and how it would affect favorably each town, each school, each family, each child. The third lecture was to show the beneficent results of the State normal schools.

By this time you are naturally and reasonably asking what was Prussian system and what did Mr. Brooks find to say in his three lectures of two hours each. He has preserved records of his having delivered them repeatedly, separately and in series. The manuscripts themselves have not been found, but by anticipating a little in the thread of the story, a document which Mr. Brooks drew up can be cited, as it contains in brief an exposition of the Prussian system. This document was a petition* sent to the Legislature in January, 1837, by the Halifax Convention.

By the time of this convention, for which Mr. Brooks prepared the document, he had acquired a felicity and directness of expression by reason of his long experience in presenting the subject to many audiences. The document is a long one, and from it we can extract four crisp and expressive sentences which will give at least a working idea of the system.

" The object of education is to develop all the powers, faculties, and affections of human nature in their natural order, proper time and due proportion, so that each one may occupy the exact place in the grown up character which God at first ordained in the infant constitution."

*Barnard's Journal of Education. Vol. XVII, p. 647.

CHARLES BROOKS (1795–1872).

BUST BY CRAWFORD, ROME, 1842.

Conforming to the wishes of the Brooks family, this bust was given to the Commonwealth of Massachusetts in 1892, and it has been placed appropriately in the office of the
State Board of Education, Massachusetts State House.

" He who has but half the powers (which God has bestowed on him), developed and in action, is just half as useful and half as happy as he might have been."

" The Prussian system, better than any with which we are acquainted, aims at unfolding the whole nature of man as the Creator designed; thus bringing out *all* the talent of the country, and thereby giving to every child the chance of making the most of himself."

" The Prussian system, therefore, is emphatically a Christian system. 'Love God, love man; do to others as you would that others should do to you.' These are the basis of all their instructions."

Now these citations have to do with the theory of education. But Brooks' work was practical rather than theoretical, and in the following quotation is the key to the method by which this Prussian system was to be put in practice.

" The Prussian principle seems to be this: that everything which it is desirable to have in the national character should be carefully inculcated in elementary education. . . . Over and over again have the Prussians proved that elementary education cannot be fully attained without purposely-prepared teachers. They deem these seminaries of priceless value and declare them in all their reports and laws to be fountains of their success. Out of this fact in their history has arisen the maxim, ' As is the master, so is the school.' "

You see, therefore, the outline of Mr. Brooks' plan.

1st. Elementary education is not of local concern only, but is of national importance, and the State must so recognize it.

2d. The State can best strengthen the cause of elementary education by furnishing purposely-prepared teachers, for " as is the teacher, so is the school."

3d. The State must commit the details to a Board of Education with a secretary who shall supervise and recommend.

It may be anticipating a conclusion, but it is the fact, whether stated now or later, that this outline is exactly what the Commonwealth of Massachusetts adopted in its laws, and as we have become used to them, we find it difficult to conceive of the conditions, some of which have already been described.

The system Brooks undertook to change was based first on the district, that is, that the education of the children was a matter to be cared for by the tax payers in that district. Hence, in advocating the principle that the education of the children was a concern of the State as well as of the locality, Brooks had to run counter to the feeling of local pride, for frequently a town would be subdivided into districts, each of which was independent of the others as regards its management of its schools.

Brooks stated often that he originated nothing, but that he brought to his own people what he found abroad. But this is not a fair statement of what he did. A comparison of what Dr. Julius told him on that voyage of forty-one days with the system as Brooks developed it, is indicative of how clearly and fully Brooks comprehended the defects of the educational system prevailing here.

Dr. Julius, during his tour of investigation in the United States, attended at Philadelphia a meeting of those interested in the welfare of prisoners. His remarks on education in its bearing on the prevention of crime were so well received that he was asked to allow them to be printed. It is fair to presume that he would not at that meeting state his facts any less strongly or clearly than he did to Brooks on that long voyage, so that we may regard these statements as being those on which Brooks based his enthusiasm for the Prussian system.*

" The well-known — and since Mr. Cousin published his interesting report — far-famed Prussian system of national education went properly into practice in the year 1819, and has three fundamental principles and supporting pillars.

"*First,* the creation of seminaries or schools for teachers in the

*Remarks on the relation between Education and Crime in a letter to the Rt. Rev. William White, D.D., president of the Philadelphia Society for Alleviating the Miseries of Public Prisons, by Francis Lieber, LL.D. To which are added some observations by N. H. Julius, M.D., of Hamburg, a corresponding member of the society. Published by order of the society, Philadelphia, 1835.

elementary schools, of which Prussia, with a population equal to that of the United States, has now forty-three, of the Protestant and Catholic denominations, furnishing annually from eight to nine hundred teachers, well informed and trained during three years for their future avocation.

"*Second*, Legal obligation of parents and guardians to send children under their care, unless under qualified teachers at home or in authorized private schools, to the public schools from the first day of their seventh to the last day of their fourteenth years.

"*Third*, The foundation of the whole system on a religious and moral basis, so that the first, or the first two hours of each day are directed entirely to a regular course of religious instruction, teaching, besides the reading of the Scriptures (for the Catholics, histories taken from the Bible), all the duties of man towards his Creator, the constituted authorities, and his fellow creatures, as they are inculcated by the Gospel."

It must not be inferred that because Brooks seems to have laid little stress on the need of religious training in the public schools, he was indifferent to religious training for the young. When one remembers the turmoil and confusion that history records as existing in the ecclesiastical circles of Massachusetts in 1836, when families were divided, friends and neighbors became enemies, business suffered, litigation was instituted in many instances, and strained relations were created, some of which continued almost to our time, it is significant that in the midst of the denominational strife, Brooks on Fast Day, 1836, could bring together in his church at Hingham an inter-denominational convention to consider Sunday-school work. He made the opening address, in which he dealt with the necessity of applying recognized educational methods to Sunday-school teaching. The meeting must have been a long one, but that was a characteristic of the meetings of that time. The names of twelve of the speakers are given in the report in the Hingham paper, prepared by Mr. Brooks, and among them are found Unitarian and Trinitarian Congregationalists, Baptists, and Methodists. One sentence from the report must suffice: "It seemed deeply impressed on many minds that Sabbath-schools were to be *the* means of renovating the church, of reforming society, of saving the world."*

By the autumn of 1836 Brooks had had enough experience in the presentation of his subject to enable him to formulate a definite plan of campaign, and that this plan was successful the sequel shows. The changes of the last seventy years have already been spoken of. Here is another instance, for the method Brooks adopted successfully then would hardly attract attention now, even if it did not defeat the purpose entirely. His plan was to call a convention.

First, he sent out a circular which he had carefully prepared and had printed as a broadside, containing sixteen hundred words. The date was November 10, 1836, and the convention was not to meet until December 7, nearly a month later. But communication was slow in those days.

After a brief appeal by way of introduction, he said: —

"In order that we may do something I would propose that a convention of delegates from the several towns in the county meet at Plymouth in Court Week (Wednesday, December 7, at 6 P.M.), to discuss the merits of the greatly improved modes of elementary instruction which have been in most successful operation for several years in Germany, Prussia, and other European states. This step might result in the appointment of a Board of Education. . . .

"There is one provision preparatory to a full instruction of our youth, which I deem of vast moment; I mean, a seminary for preparing teachers. After this is established, all other improvements may be easily carried forward; and until this is done, we shall, I fear, advance, but in very slow and broken steps. In Prussia there are forty-two such seminaries, and they are there found to be the very life blood of their school system, a system vastly superior to ours. Two such seminaries, one for males, and the other for females, situated, the one in Plymouth and the other in Middleboro, would soon have a direct influence on every school in the county."

He then mentions in detail topics that might be discussed to advantage in meetings called officially by the Board of Education, such as schoolhouses and their construction, school books, compulsory attendance, and the

*Hingham Gazette, April 15, 1836.

prevention of truancy, the teaching of singing and drawing and other features which are today taken as matters of course, thanks to the adoption of the tried and proved Prussian system he advocated.

But Brooks inspired others with his own enthusiasm, as this quotation shows: —

"I sent copies of this circular, printed on letter paper, to each board of selectmen, each school committee, and each clergyman in the county, requesting clergymen to read it on the next Sunday to their people. Most of them read it. The circular was kindly noticed by the leading newspapers of the State. The large meeting-house of the First Parish in Plymouth was filled, and I opened the whole matter as clearly and strongly as I could, showing that the great work must begin by founding a State normal school in Plymouth County.

"I invited the audience to catechize me as much as they could about my views and plans, and they did so. The audience warmed themselves up, and Ichabod Morton, Esq., Deacon of the First Parish, rose and said, 'Mr. President, I am glad to see this day. The work is well begun. The mass of facts now presented to us so plainly, prove conclusively the inestimable value of teachers' seminaries. Mr. Brooks says he wants the first one established in the Old Colony, and so do I, sir, and I will give one thousand dollars towards its establishment.'

"I knew that the generous offer of this humble and pious man* would do more for my cause than all my lectures, and I therefore secured a notice of it in every newspaper in Massachusetts. Thus my client, the Prussian stranger, began its journey from the Plymouth Rock."†

The convention after two days' session, adopted resolutions endorsing Mr. Brooks' views. At all the conventions Mr. Brooks attended and where he spoke, it

* Hon. Wm. T. Davis of Plymouth has kindly furnished some facts about this enthusiastic co-adjutor of Brooks. Ichabod Morton, born in Plymouth, was a descendant of George Morton, the father of Nathaniel, the first secretary of the Plymouth Colony. His education was slight, for he became engaged early in the work of life; first, as clerk in, and then keeper of, a country store. As he had learned something of surveying, he would at times survey wood lots. His store keeping led to an interest in vessels, first in the Grand Bank fishing, and afterwards with larger vessels in the coasting and West India trade. Like all traders, in his early days he sold rum and other liquors, but at the institution of the temperance movement in Plymouth, he advertised September 8, 1827, on behalf of his firm "That prolific mother of miseries, that giant foe to human happiness, shall no longer have a dwelling under our roof."

Feeling his own lack of early education, he was always advocating in town meeting increased appropriations for schools. He joined the anti-slavery movement in 1835, and when Brook Farm was established, he became a member and built a house there. His business interests at Plymouth naturally suffered by this, but he returned to them with more zeal than ever. He had six sons and a daughter, Mrs. Abby Morton Diaz, the author of the William Henry letters.

† Address at Framingham.

was his custom to have resolutions adopted, and these resolutions he prepared beforehand, so there was a unanimity in the demands. This Plymouth convention was followed in quick succession during December by others at Hingham, Duxbury, New Bedford, Fairhaven and Bridgewater. Evidently there was then no Christmas rush. He must have been satisfied with the response at these meetings, for again he calls another convention; this time it is for the specific purpose of securing for the Old Colony a seminary for teachers. The call was dated January 5, 1837, and was for a convention at Halifax on January 24, 1837.

But after this call was issued and before the convention was held, a couple of events happened which satisfied Mr. Brooks that his work had not been in vain. The first was the interrogative statement in the governor's message as to whether it would not be well to arrange for a school commission. The second event was an invitation from the Legislature that Mr. Brooks deliver an address before them on schools. Hear his own words on this : —

"One evening in January, 1837, I was sitting reading to my family when a letter was brought me from the friends of education in the Massachusetts Legislature, asking me to lecture on my hobby subject. I was electrified with joy. The whole heavens, to my eyes, seemed now filled with rainbows. January 18 came, and the hall of the House of Representatives was perfectly full. I gave an account of the Prussian system, and they asked if I would lecture again. I consented, and the next evening endeavored to show how far the Prussian system could be safely adopted in the United States."*

The Halifax convention voted to adopt a petition to the Legislature which Mr. Brooks drew up, and which the chairman and secretary signed, praying for a teachers' seminary in Plymouth County.† This petition sets forth at length the arguments Brooks used in his lectures, and it is worth a careful study.

*Old Colony Memorial newspaper, October 4, 1845.
†Hingham Gazette, February 24, 1837.

Rev. Chs. Brooks,

My dear Sir,

The new Normal
school house at Bridge-
water is to be dedicated on
Wednesday the 19th a. int.
— Address by Hon. Wm G,
Reb,

Your name is so
peculiarly associated
with Normal Schools, that
a Dedication would not
be without danger of being
set aside as spurious &
invalid, if you were not
present, Tho' we expect
to have a pleasant time,
yet we can hardly afford

to go this' with it again, & therefore we hope it will be legitimated by your presence,

Very truly & sincerely
Yours &c
Horace Mann

Wrentham Aug. 12. 1846.

Rev. Chs. Brooks,

      My dear Sir,

          The new Normal School house at Bridgewater is to be dedicated on Wednesday the 19th inst., address by Hon. Wm. G. Bates.

   Your name is so familiarly associated with Normal Schools, that a Dedication would not be without danger of being set aside as spurious & invalid, if you were not present. Tho' we expect to have a pleasant time, yet we can hardly afford to go thro' with it again, & therefore we hope it will be legitimated by your presence.

                    Very truly & sincerely,
                        Yours
                        Horace Mann.

Wrentham Aug. 12, 1846.

Two months later, in April, 1837, the act* establishing the Board of Education was signed by Governor Edward Everett, and now Horace Mann comes into the story of the movement, for he was appointed secretary for the board. This appointment was unexpected to him and to others, for Mr. Brooks and others who knew and appreciated what James G. Carter had been doing for fourteen years, advocated his appointment. It is thought that Edmund Dwight, of whom we shall hear more presently, was responsible for Mann's appointment. There has never been any question that whoever it was that secured the appointment of Horace Mann to this important office, it was wise, discreet, and a tribute to someone's knowledge of men, for later events showed that Mann was emphatically the one for the place.

Until the date of Mann's appointment he had had nothing to do with the cause to which he gave so much, and on which his fame rests, except some experience as a tutor and one term as school committee man in Dedham. He was a lawyer in active practice. He had recently completed printing a revision of the statutes of Massachusetts and was serving a second term as president of the Senate when the act was passed establishing the Board of Education. What he did, what he endured, what attacks he had to meet, what financial sacrifices he made, all are matters of record, and his fame is secure.

Brooks says that he thought that now it was time for him to return to his professional duties, as that for which he had labored had been accomplished when the board was created. But Mann urged him to keep on with his lecturing until normal schools were secured. Brooks replied that they *were* secured, now that the board had been established. Brooks, however, did continue, for the movement had acquired such great momentum that he was needed to guide it by explaining just what was needed.

*Acts of 1837, Chap. 241. An Act relating to Common Schools. The secretary shall diffuse information of educational methods " to the end that all children in this Commonwealth, who depend upon common schools for instruction, may have the best education which those schools can be made to impart."

Up and down the state he went, two thousand miles in his chaise, and over into New Hampshire and Vermont, Rhode Island, Connecticut, New York and Pennsylvania, ever ringing the changes on his maxim : " As is the teacher, so is the school," stating the facts about what the system had actually wrought in Prussia, and urging the people to adopt the same successful system here.

When the Legislature met in January, 1838, the next winter after the Board of Education had been established, the subject of normal schools was in the air and something had to be done. The Legislature wished to hear arguments, and Horace Mann, as secretary, first addressed them. The second address was by Mr. Brooks on Normal Schools and School Reform. The governor's message recommended normal schools, and when a private citizen anonymously, through Horace Mann as secretary, offered the Commonwealth of Massachusetts ten thousand dollars for normal schools if the Legislature would appropriate an equal amount, the act was passed. On April 19, 1838, the gift was accepted, the appropriation made, and normal schools began their course. The donor of the ten thousand dollars was Edmund Dwight,* a Boston merchant.

In addition to his general lecturing, Brooks worked for a normal school in Plymouth County. In September, 1838, a convention of the Plymouth County Association for the improvement of schools was held at Hanover to urge the establishment of a normal school in Plymouth County. Mr. Brooks saw the importance of the meeting and of the thoughts brought out, for later he had an abstract of the speeches printed for circulation. To this meeting† Brooks succeeded in bringing as speakers, Horace Mann, Rev. Dr. George Putnam, Robert Rantoul, Jr., President John Quincy Adams and Daniel Webster. Mr. Adams had previously declined, giving as his reason his ignorance of the subject, but

*Memoir of Edmund Dwight, by Francis Bowen. Barnard's Journal of Education, Vol. IV, p. 14.
†Barnard's Journal of Education. Vol. I, p. 587, has a full report of the meeting.

Mr. Brooks wanted him and induced him to come. Adams, "the old man eloquent," was then deep in his contests over petitions to Congress.

Mr. Adams' speech shows that he had learned much at the convention. Among other points he made was this: "We see monarchs expending vast sums in educating the children of their poorest subjects, and shall we be outdone by kings?"

Daniel Webster, the old reporter said, "addressed the assembly for half an hour in his usual style of eloquence." One of his statements must be noted: "Teachers should teach things. It is a reproach that the public schools are not superior to the private. If I had as many sons as old Priam, I would send them all to the public schools."

With such speakers and with the changes rung on the old theme of Plymouth Rock and the Old Colony, it is evident that any action a convention with such features might take, would carry weight. The demand was that a normal school be located in Plymouth County. One was eventually established at Bridgewater, but instead of being the first, it was the third. With this convention, Mr. Brooks' immediate labors ceased.

About this time his name was suggested for the professorship of natural history in the University of the City of New York. His brilliant work in aid of the educational cause was well known, and that alone should have secured him the appointment, but in addition, he had the endorsement of four such men as Jared Sparks, Edward Everett, Josiah Quincy and John Quincy Adams. On receiving the appointment, he prepared to close his labors in Hingham, and the pastorate was terminated January 1, 1839, after eighteen years of service.

If this paper were to end with this incident, the point made some time ago would be emphasized; namely, Mr. Brooks' work had a definite beginning and a definite ending. Possibly your interest, however, may be sufficient to cause you to ask as to his later life. On receiving the appointment to this post, for which he had had no special training, he entered upon a preparation. As the best place for study of the subject was Paris, he went abroad September, 1839, and there remained four years. I have not learned whether on his return, in 1843, he entered actively upon the duties of his position. If he did, it was for but a short time, for through failing eyesight, he was compelled to resign. One result of this foreign study was the compilation of a text-book entitled "Elements of Ornithology," a copy of which he gave to the library at Harvard University.

Two years later, that is, 1845, we find him on the Boston school committee, and, as usual, active in the work. In 1848, still carrying out his old desire to *do* something concerning a cause which aroused sympathy, he instituted the Society for the Relief of Aged and Destitute Clergymen, of which he, with Francis Parkman and Ephraim Peabody, were the incorporators, in 1850. That society now has funds of nearly two hundred thousand dollars, and is aiding twenty beneficiaries in sums varying from one to five hundred dollars a year. The name has lately been changed from that given by Brooks, and is now the Society for Ministerial Relief.

In 1853, he printed a small slip on colored paper, announcing the preparation of a History of Medford, which was published two years later, in 1855. The press comments are preserved in the scrap book. At the same time, his attention was directed to what was probably a new subject of study, " The Evil Results following the Marriage of Near Blood Relatives. With his thoroughness, he gathered many instances, and published and spoke. The scrap book contains an interesting account of an address by him in Providence, in 1855. The reporter was a trifle facetious, and this facetiousness did not tend to lessen the attacks made on Brooks through the columns of a paper printed in one of the localities mentioned. Here is what the reporter made Mr. Brooks say: —

CHARLES BROOKS (1795–1872).

Photographed by Whipple, Boston, 1861.

"Inhabitants of the Bahamas haven't much brains and are homely as sin. Reason, they intermarry. At Martha's Vineyard, they have a particularly bad time. The island is sea girt. The youths cannot go courting elsewhere because of the rolling billows, and so they content themselves with Marthas in the Vineyard. The island is in consequence, according to our author, full of illustrations. Their minds," says Mr. Brooks, mildly, "are moderate. Their health is feeble."

From this time on he was frequently called upon for addresses on education, and he apparently still retained his power to attract and charm his audiences. It was his custom, when addressing schools, to teach the children what he called his formula. Some of those who in childhood were taught it, have asked that it be preserved.

"Children should be taught in school what they will most need in the world." So say the Prussians. Therefore learn

1. To live religiously.
2. To think comprehensively.
3. To reckon mathematically.
4. To converse elegantly.
5. To write grammatically.

The last great work, or perhaps I had better say, the last of his special labors calling for his activity, was in the line of his work of thirty years previous. He worked very hard on behalf of a National Board of Education. By this time he was seventy years of age, but yet he wrote for the press, spoke in public, corresponded with members of Congress, and made journeys to Washington in advocacy of the cause. Letters have been found from Sumner, Banks, Boutwell, Garfield, Winthrop, and others, all of which show that he put his case in such a way as to receive attention. The measure as passed by Congress shows that a National Board of Education was established along the same lines that he urged the State of Massachusetts to adopt thirty years before; namely, education is a matter of national concern. After this, he seems to have lived in retirement and an honored old age. He died at Medford, July 7, 1872, nearly seventy-seven years of age, leaving one son who died unmarried, in 1885.

It is doubtful if again an attempt will be made to prepare a paper on the work of Charles Brooks for Normal Schools. It seems, therefore, that I should submit to you at this time what is the conclusion of my delving as an "educational antiquary," a personification of Mr. Brooks' fancy of sixty years ago.

There are three men who will stand out above others in the history of that time: Carter, who showed the need; Brooks, who offered the remedy and aroused public attention so that the law was established, and Horace Mann, who put the law into practice.

At the Framingham meeting in July, 1864, one of the orators prepared an historical sketch of the labors of the men of the fourth decade of the century, and described what each had done. Of Brooks, he said: —

" To Charles Brooks, whose labors in the years 1835–6–7 were second to those of no man—one might also say to no number of men — we owe the particular *form* which normal schools took, and he did very much toward preparing the public mind to look with favor on the new system. From his friend, Victor Cousin, the first scholar of France, he obtained reports and documents, and encouraging words which were to him the *pabulum vitae;* for in this phase of the enterprise he stood almost, if not quite alone; yet planting his feet literally on Plymouth Rock, he was conscious of strength.*

Brooks waived for himself all claim to originating any policy. He found the Prussian system, urged its adoption, and the Commonwealth of Massachusetts made it a law. For over ten years, James Carter had been working, but had made little progress. His field was among educators in the American Institute of Instruction, and later in the Legislature, where he did grand work. But the people had not been aroused, and in this particular and important field Brooks labored.

To his audiences Brooks was a man of attractive presence, a cultured gentleman, thoroughly unselfish, plainly influenced by a desire to benefit children, reinforcing his arguments with appeals to his hearers' patri-

*Barnard's Journal of Education, Vol. XVII, p. 664. Historical Sketch by Rev. Eben S. Stearns.

otism and Christianity. Could there be any other effect than that the hearers should carry away pleasing remembrances of the speaker and the cause?

To those who were brought into closer contact in the discussion, whether public or private, that was sure to follow his address, he showed himself a man of tact, energy, enthusiasm, and of unwavering faith that what had succeeded elsewhere would succeed here. And so he went, hither and yon, making friends for himself and friends for the cause, and the result was shown when the matter came before the Legislature; and Carter, then a member, found his years of pleading strengthened with the support of legislators who were responsive to the wishes of their constituents, Brooks' friends.

Mann took up the work where Brooks laid it down, and to him fell the application of the remedy Brooks had shown, and with this application went also the antagonism, yes, the contumely of those to whom the advance in education brought discomfort. Mann's work is recorded in detail in many places. Let there be also recorded the work of the man who brought the support of the public; the high-minded, the self-sacrificing man of charming personality — Charles Brooks.